NEW ZEALAND
LAND OF THE LONG WHITE CLOUD

DISCOVERING our HERITAGE

by Valerie Keyworth

dP | DILLON PRESS, INC.
Minneapolis, Minnesota 55415

Acknowledgments

I would like to thank the following people for their information and assistance: Tania Burroughs; the staff of the New Zealand Consulate General; and the staff of the Blanchard Community Library in Santa Paula, California.

The photographs are reproduced through the courtesy of Cameramann International; The New Zealand Film Commission; the New Zealand Tourist & Publicity Office; John Penisten; and E.W. Young/Tom Stack & Associates. Cover photograph by John Penisten.

Library of Congress Cataloging-in-Publication Data

Keyworth, Valerie.
New Zealand : land of the long white cloud / Valerie Keyworth.
p. cm. — (Discovering our heritage)
Bibliography: p.
Includes index.
Summary: Discusses the history, people, religions, geography, festivals, food, and folk tales of the South Pacific nation.
ISBN 0-87518-414-6 : $12.95
1. New Zealand—Juvenile literature. [1. New Zealand.]
I. Title. II. Series.
DU408.K48 1990
993—dc20   89-11716
                                                  CIP
                                                  AC

Dillon Press, Inc., 242 Portland Avenue South
Minneapolis, Minnesota 55415

Printed in the United States of America
1 2 3 4 5 6 7 8 9 10 99 98 97 96 95 94 93 92 91 90

Contents

Fast Facts about New Zealand

Official Name: New Zealand.

Capital: Wellington.

Location: New Zealand is an island nation located in the southwestern Pacific Ocean. It is 6,500 miles (10,465 kilometers) southwest of the United States and about 1,000 miles (1,610 kilometers) southeast of Australia. The Tasman Sea separates New Zealand from Australia.

Area: 103,515 square miles (268,104 square kilometers). The North Island covers 44, 244 square miles (114,592 square kilometers), and the South Island covers 58,965 square miles (152,719 square kilometers). These two main islands extend more than 1,000 miles (1,610 kilometers) in length, with a total coastline of more than 3,200 miles (5,152 kilometers).

Elevation: *Highest*—Mount Cook, 12,349 feet (3,766 meters) above sea level. *Lowest*—sea level along the coast.

Population: *Estimated 1988 population*—3,372,000. *Distribution*—82 percent of the people live in or near cities; 18 percent live in rural areas. *Density*—32 persons per square mile (13 per square kilometer).

Form of Government: Parliamentary system with one house, the House of Representatives. Great Britain's Queen Elizabeth II is the head of state, and a prime minister is the head of government.

Important Products: Lamb and beef, wool, dairy products, forest products, fruit.

Basic Unit of Money: New Zealand dollar.

Official Languages: English, Maori.

Major Religions: Church of England, Presbyterian, Roman Catholic.

Flag: New Zealand's flag has a dark blue background with a small British flag in the top left-hand corner. Four red stars to the right form the constellation of the Southern Cross.

National Anthems: "God Defend New Zealand" (national); "God Save the Queen" (royal).

Major Holidays: New Year's Day—January 1; New Zealand or Waitangi Day—February 6; Good Friday, Easter, Easter Monday (dates vary); ANZAC Day, April 25; Queen's Birthday—first Monday in June; Labour Day—fourth Monday in October; Christmas Day—December 25; Boxing Day—December 26.

Ninety
Mile
Beach

Bay of Islands

Russell

Auckland

Ngaruawahia

Hamilton

Waikato River

Rotorua

Wanganui River

Gisborne

North Island

Tasman Sea

Wellington

Cook Strait

NEW ZEALAND

South Island

Pacific Ocean

Southern Alps

Mount
Cook

Canterbury Plains

Christchurch

Milford
Sound

Queenstown

Lake
Wakatipu

Otago

Dunedin

Foveaux Strait

Stewart
Island

NORTH
AMERICA

EUROPE

ASIA

AFRICA

SOUTH
AMERICA

AUSTRALIA

NEW ZEALAND

N

1. An Island Country

Far away in the South Pacific Ocean and isolated from the rest of the world, lies a beautiful island country named *Aotearoa*. This means "land of the long white cloud" in the language of the *Maoris*, the first settlers on the islands. To the rest of the world, it is better known as New Zealand.

The country is famous the world over for its spectacular scenery. New Zealand's blue-green lakes, crashing waterfalls, snow-capped mountains, and hilly, green pastures spotted with sheep impress all who see them.

New Zealand has more than a wealth of natural beauty. It is known, too, for its tradition of equal rights. Maoris, the native people, and *Pakehas*—the Maori word for white people—are equal and united today. Old barriers are being broken down, to help all citizens be successful in careers, education, and politics. This small country shows concern for the welfare of all its people.

South of the Equator

The group of hilly, green islands that makes up New Zealand lies between the Tasman Sea and the

These New Zealanders enjoy the surf on one of their many sandy beaches, Cathedral Cove Beach.

Pacific Ocean. Australia is New Zealand's closest neighbor, but, in fact, it is not close at all. New Zealand lies about 1,000 miles (1,610 kilometers) southeast of Australia.

From north to south, New Zealand is 1,000 miles long. No point in the country is farther than 70 miles (112 kilometers) from the sea. The country's long, narrow shape gives it many beaches and sheltered bays. Scenic views of sandy beaches and snow-capped mountains are a natural gift that New Zealanders enjoy from almost any point on their homeland.

New Zealand has two main bodies of land—North Island and South Island. Several dozen other islands belong to the country, but many of these are hundreds of miles away. They include the Chatham Islands (528 miles or 850 kilometers east of South Island) and a section of Antarctica called the Ross Dependency. The Tokelau Islands, also in the South Pacific Ocean, are governed by New Zealand.

Because New Zealand lies south of the equator, its climatic patterns are opposite from those in the United States. The northern parts of the country are subtropical, with rainfall common throughout the year. Farther south, the climate is cooler, and the winters are cold and snowy. This land's seasons are upside-down, too. Summer lasts from December to March, and winter lasts from June until September.

New Zealand lies on an earthquake fault line, a break in the earth's crust, or upper layer. Each year about two hundred earthquakes shake the land.

South Island

South Island is famous for its magnificent mountain ranges, glaciers, sweeping plains, and beautiful fiords—narrow sea inlets that flow between steep, rocky

Hikers rest in Hooker Valley on South Island and view the breathtaking scene of Mount Cook.

cliffs. This is New Zealand's largest body of land. The snow-capped Southern Alps run down the middle of South Island. In the heart of the Southern Alps is Mount Cook, New Zealand's highest mountain. Mount Cook is 12,349 feet (3,766 meters) high. Maoris called the mountain *Aorangi*, "the Cloud Piercer."

To the east of Mount Cook, on the edge of the vast

Canterbury Plains, lies the city of Christchurch. This city looks very English, with its cathedral, bicyclists, and Avon River, which flows through the heart of town. If Christchurch is New Zealand's most English city, then Dunedin is its most Scottish. Dunedin lies south of Christchurch along the eastern coast.

Northwest of Dunedin is Queenstown, a popular ski resort. It overlooks Lake Wakatipu, or "the Lake that Breathes." The waters of the *S*-shaped lake rise and fall three inches (7.6 centimeters) every fifteen minutes. Maori legends say this is caused by the pulsing of a giant's heart at the bottom of the lake. Scientists say it is due to the wind and changes in the atmosphere.

Across the Foveaux Strait from South Island is New Zealand's Stewart Island. This tiny body of land is only forty-five miles (seventy-two kilometers) long. Just 500 people live on Stewart Island year-round. But every year they are joined by more than 40,000 tourists. The island's main town is Oban, on Halfmoon Bay. Stewart Islanders make their living by fishing and tending to their many tourists.

North Island

North Island is a place of big cities. It is also a place of hot pools, volcanoes, and deep forest. Three-fourths of New Zealand's 3.3 million people live here. The weather is milder in the north, and more jobs are available in North Island's large cities. The narrow peninsula in the far north, called Northland, is New Zealand's citrus-growing region.

Auckland, located on North Island, is the nation's largest city and the leading business center. It is a cultural center, too, with galleries, theaters, and museums that attract New Zealanders and tourists alike. Built on top of a series of ancient volcanoes, Auckland is a bustling, modern city.

South of Auckland is the city of Hamilton and New Zealand's main dairy farming region. Southwest of Hamilton, near the town of Rotorua, rests a huge underground bed of hot water and steam. Holes are dug deep in the earth to tap the steam. It is then piped to a powerhouse to make electricity.

Some steam naturally escapes in this area and drifts over the land. The smell of sulfur, a scent like rotten eggs, hangs in the air. Next to pools of bubbling mud, geysers shoot skyward, some as high as 100 feet (30.5 meters).

To the west of Rotorua are the Waitomo Caves and the Glow Worm Grotto. These two places are among the most magical on North Island. Over the centuries, the Waitomo Caves have formed from limestone. Glistening structures fill the caves, created by water dripping from the ceilings. Glow Worm Grotto is a cavern lighted

The steamy region of Rotorua.

by thousands of lights that look like tiny blue stars. The spots of light are really glowworms (firefly grubs) that glow in the dark.

New Zealand's capital, Wellington, lies at the southern end of North Island. Hilly and windy, Wellington is often compared to San Francisco. Flat land space is scarce in this city, and many of the houses have been built on the sides of hills. A big attraction in the capital is a circular building called the Beehive. The Beehive

The Beehive in Wellington, the nation's capital.

contains busy people, not bees. It holds the offices of New Zealand's government officials.

City Dwellers

Most New Zealanders choose to live in their country's bustling cities rather than on their land's rugged countryside. Four-fifths of New Zealanders are city dwellers. A million people live in or around the city of Auckland. That is nearly one-third of New Zealand's total population.

Lights blaze on Auckland's skyline and the Auckland Harbour Bridge as evening falls. One million New Zealanders have chosen Auckland as their home.

New Zealand's cities are busy places, but not as crowded as American cities. Most city dwellers live in houses with private gardens, rather than in high-rise apartment buildings. Compared to major American urban centers, New Zealand's are orderly and quiet.

Cities also serve as the nation's main manufacturing centers. Their factories produce electronics, textiles, and clothing, as well as leather goods, rubber goods, plastics, pottery, glassware, and furniture.

Whether they live in the city or the country, most New Zealanders enjoy a satisfactory standard of living. Almost every family owns a car. More than half of the families own private homes, furnished with modern appliances.

Farm Folk

New Zealand's main exports come from rural areas rather than the cities. The nation's hilly countryside is not easy to farm with machinery, but it is perfect for sheep and cattle grazing. This small country is the world's biggest exporter of lamb, dairy products, and mutton—the meat of full-grown sheep. In fact, the country has twenty-five times as many farm animals as people! New Zealand is also the world's second largest exporter of wool.

New Zealand's sheep ranches are called stations. Most stations and farms are run by families. A farm family's nearest neighbors may be miles away. Many farm children go to boarding schools to get an education, and to meet other children their own age.

Member of the Commonwealth

New Zealand is a member of the Commonwealth of Nations. This is an association of countries that were

An Angora goat. Most of the country's wool comes from sheep, but the Angora goat's silky wool is a growing export in New Zealand.

once part of the British Empire, but now choose to work together. Britain's Queen Elizabeth II is New Zealand's head of state. This position is symbolic, rather than one with any decision-making power.

New Zealand is governed by a parliamentary system with only one chamber, the House of Representatives. Ninety-seven members belong to this house; four are Maori members elected by Maori voters. The head of government is the prime minister, the leader of the political party that receives the most votes.

New Zealand joins foreign countries to promote trade and peace worldwide. It contributes to United Nations assistance programs and has its own aid programs to help the islands of the South Pacific. This small, faraway nation is an active and helpful member of the world community.

2. *"She'll Be Right, Mate!"*

When situations turn sour or seem impossible, New Zealanders often say in their casual British accent, "She'll be right, mate!" This saying means that whatever is wrong will right itself with time.

New Zealanders are known for finding solutions to problems. They are strong believers in equal rights and solve many problems by paying close attention to the needs of their citizens. Although the cultures of some of their citizens differ a great deal, New Zealanders have worked actively to promote peace on their islands.

Relations between the Maoris and Europeans who immigrate to New Zealand have not always been peaceful. Most of New Zealand's 3.3 million citizens are descendants of people from Great Britain and other countries in Europe. More than 400,000 of the islands' citizens are Maori. Smaller numbers of Asians and immigrants from other Pacific islands—the Cook Islands, Tonga, Western Samoa, Niue Island, and the Tokelau Islands—make up the rest of the nation's population. Most New Zealanders value their different cultures and backgrounds. They are proud of their shared culture and of the strides they have made to become part of the world community.

Maori and other New Zealand children are from different cultures but grow up sharing common interests, including the love of rugby.

A Nation of Kiwis

New Zealanders are all united under the nickname "Kiwi." New Zealanders borrowed their nickname from the famous flightless bird, the kiwi. The small kiwi bird (about the size of a hen) is native to New Zealand. Since the kiwi has stumps instead of wings it can't fly, but it can run quite fast. New Zealanders regard the flightless kiwi as their national bird.

New Zealanders named one of their most popular crops and exports after their national bird—the kiwi

The kiwi, New Zealand's national bird.

fruit. The kiwi fruit is brown and fuzzy on the outside, and emerald-green and delicious on the inside. The kiwi fruit is popular in making salads and pies. New Zealand is the leading producer of this tasty fruit.

A flightless bird, an enjoyable fruit, and even this country's people go by the name kiwi. New Zealand is famous the world over for being a nation of kiwis.

A Self-Made Land

New Zealanders have a reputation for being great

do-it-yourselfers. They enjoy building or redecorating their homes, or working in their gardens.

This do-it-yourself nature stems from the days of the early settlers, who worked to build a homeland in spite of rugged land and a sometimes harsh climate. Long periods of rainy weather kept the settlers indoors, and they had to invent their own entertainment. The long distances that goods traveled from Europe meant a shortage of ready-made supplies. Instead of buying supplies, the pioneers had to create their own. Today, the New Zealand dollar does not go very far when buying foreign-made goods, and the goods are often too expensive to purchase. Instead, New Zealanders try to be creative and build, sew, and invent what they need. These do-it-yourself people are known for their handicrafts, such as pottery, leather work, and hand-knit sweaters.

Because New Zealanders have to work hard for what they have, their homeland is not a throw-away society. Many old items are saved, used again, or recycled. One way that New Zealanders have learned about conservation is through the lesson of the kauri tree. Many of the early settlers were attracted to New Zealand by the vast forests of huge kauri trees. The Maoris made canoes out of the trees. But with the coming of the pioneers, European shipbuilders began to make ship masts out of the kauris' tall trunks. In a matter of decades, the forests turned into bare fields. The kauri could not be replaced since it required as long as 1,000 years to grow. Today, remaining kauris can be seen at Waipoua State Forest in Northland. The tallest tree stands 167 feet (51 meters) tall and is about 1,200 years old.

Equal Rights

New Zealand is known as a country that cares for its citizens equally. The country's laws guarantee that every person has the right to a job, a place to live, health care, and an education. This tradition began with the early settlers, who came to New Zealand to get away from the slums and class structure of Europe. The settlers wanted a new life where everyone—man or woman, rich or poor—could be free from worry over misfortunes such as sickness and unemployment.

New Zealanders receive large health and financial benefits from the government. Public hospital and emergency care is free, and part of the cost of visiting a doctor is paid by the government. Anyone who cannot work for a time because of illness or injury may receive a payment to make up for lost wages. Single parents receive financial help in supporting the cost of raising their children. People who are older than sixteen and cannot find work may receive an unemployment benefit.

A Maori man operates computerized cheese packaging machinery in one of New Zealand's dairy companies.

Since all of these benefits are financed by taxes, New Zealand's taxes are fairly high. Tax money is not always enough, however, and many programs depend on volunteers to help out. Many New Zealanders offer their time and energy to help their less fortunate neighbors.

It is common to see children and adults spend their weekends collecting money for charity. Some organizations are staffed and run by volunteers. One of these is the Saint John's Ambulance Association, which runs 70 percent of New Zealand's free ambulance services.

Unity through the Arts

New Zealanders believe that to live in harmony, they must bring together the different cultures of their people. One exciting result of this blend is the nation's rich mix of art forms.

Perhaps the most exciting artwork in New Zealand has been created by the Maoris. Many New Zealanders feel that if it were not for the wealth of Maori legends, songs, and dances, the country's culture would be very ordinary indeed.

The Maoris have a long history of creating skilled crafts, which are best shown in their carving. Maori carvings have flowing, curved lines and masterful use of inlaid *paua* shell. Each piece of carved wood or greenstone, the New Zealand jade, tells a story or represents an ancestor, god, or myth. Maoris first used their dramatic designs to decorate meetinghouses, canoes, tools, weapons, and jewelry. Today, Maori spiral patterns are also used in advertising, such as the Air New Zealand symbol. Maori designs are seen in everyday places, too, such as on the edge of an airmail envelope. A careful eye can spot Maori designs all over New Zealand.

New Zealand's poets and novelists work to blend

Examples of skilled, detailed Maori carvings are seen all over New Zealand.

cultures through art forms, too. In 1985, Keri Hulme's novel *The Bone People* received the Booker McConnell prize, one of the world's highest literary awards, for its insight into present-day Maori problems. Maori artists and writers, such as Selwyn Muru and Witi Ihimaera, have taken traditional Maori subjects—myths and people, for instance—and given them a new setting in the city. Fantasy writer Hugh Cook and award-winning children's author Margaret Mahy include many Maori images in their books.

The poet James K. Baxter believed strongly that Maoris and European New Zealanders should understand and appreciate each other's cultures. He dedicated his life to bridging the gap between them. At his home on the Wanganui River in New Zealand, Baxter gave troubled Maori and white young people a place to gather and resolve their differences.

Most New Zealanders feel that their country's future success depends on this blending of cultures. Today, schoolchildren are taught the Maori language as a standard subject. Radio and television news programs are now broadcast in both English and Maori. More and more, Maoris and New Zealanders of European heritage are raising families comfortable in both cultures. With sharing, caring, and positive attitudes from all New Zealanders, these citizens believe, "She'll be right, mate!"

3. Newcomers to an Old Nation

No one knows for certain when people first lived in what is now New Zealand. Most New Zealanders believe that the Maoris were the first. Historians agree that the greatest number of Maoris probably traveled to present-day New Zealand in a great migration from Polynesia about A.D. 1350. Since the weather was milder on North Island, most of the Maori nation settled there.

The Maoris lived mainly by hunting, fishing, and growing vegetables. These people were also highly skilled woodcarvers and created elaborate carvings with stone tools. The early Maoris hunted the large, flightless *moa* for food. These ostrich-like birds were enormous, sometimes growing twelve feet (3.6 meters) tall! The Maoris hunted the moa until it disappeared. The bird is now extinct, but the Maoris depended on it for survival centuries ago.

Many years later, in 1642, the first European to sight New Zealand was a Dutch explorer, Abel Tasman. Tasman did not go ashore, but named the land Staten Landt and marked it on his map. Dutch geographers later renamed Staten Landt *New Zealand* after a Dutch province, but no one showed any interest in going there again for many years.

Captain James Cook landed on North Island in 1769.

More than 100 years later, in 1769, Captain James Cook became the first European to explore New Zealand. His expedition sailed completely around the two main islands and charted their coastlines. Cook's findings encouraged adventurers to seek their fortunes in the new lands. Whalers and sealers built isolated settlements on North Island and along the west coast of

South Island. They established headquarters for their whaling fleets where the town of Russell in the Bay of Islands is today.

Guns and Missionaries

Centuries ago, in the language of the Maoris, *maori* meant "normal" or "everyday," not the name of a people. Tribal names such as Te Arawa or Ngati Haua were used instead. There were many different tribes within the Maori race. Often, these tribes had disagreements that erupted into war.

Maori battles were fought hand to hand with spears or a sharp-edged stone club called a *patu*, and were usually settled quickly. War was like an art form to the Maoris. Skill and bravery in battle were praised and many dances and legends celebrated their glory.

When whalers introduced guns to the Maoris, the native people's method of warfare changed. With guns, Maoris fought each other more than ever before. The effects were terrible. Wounds from musketballs led to infections which the Maoris could not cure. This constant fighting, combined with diseases caught from the whalers, killed thousands of Maoris. Drinking the whalers' alcohol made many of the people ill and depressed; they stopped hunting and growing food. Together, these problems threatened to destroy the entire Maori race.

Years ago in Maori culture, dances, legends, and carvings cele-brated the bravery of tribal warriors.

By the late 1830s, about two thousand traders, whalers, and missionaries lived on the islands of New Zealand. Much of the missionaries' work was undone by the whalers' drunken, violent behavior. The missionaries asked Britain for help and protection against these wild men. They called for law and order, asking that New Zealand become a British colony.

The Treaty of Waitangi

Back in England, other people became interested in moving to New Zealand. A young man, Edward Gibbon Wakefield, developed a plan for starting a model colony in New Zealand. He sold people plots of land before they left England. Wakefield's first settlers landed in Wellington Harbour on January 22, 1840.

British officials realized that the growing number of settlers in New Zealand needed a government. Captain William Hobson was sent to claim New Zealand as a British colony. The islands were to become part of the Australian colony of New South Wales, and Captain Hobson was to be its lieutenant-governor. To do this, he first had to make the arrangements official by signing a treaty with the Maoris.

The treaty asked that the Maoris recognize Britain's Queen Victoria as their ruler. If they did, they would own their land and have the full rights of English citizens. The treaty stated that Maoris could keep control of their land and could sell it only to the British government, not directly to the settlers. In the Maori culture, however, land was never "sold." They believed that the earth was alive, with its own spirit. It was not something a person could own.

After several days of heated discussions between British officials and Maori leaders, some of the leaders thought they finally understood the terms. They agreed to sign the treaty on February 6, 1840. The treaty later became known as the Treaty of Waitangi, and in May 1840, New Zealand became a British colony.

Today, many Maoris and Pakehas—the Maori name for white New Zealanders—feel that this treaty was not fully fair or legal. Not all of the Maori leaders agreed to sign the treaty. Also, many New Zealanders believe that parts of the treaty were not completely understood by the Maori leaders who did sign it. For instance, it was never clearly explained to them that the government could resell the land to future settlers. The signing of this misunderstood treaty would lead to war.

Settlement Leads to War

In 1841, New Zealand was declared a colony independent of New South Wales. Trying to grow food in the colony's early days was very difficult. Sometimes the

The signing of the Treaty of Waitangi.

settlers could not farm enough land to feed even themselves; only buying food from the Maoris kept them alive. In 1844, life improved when two flocks of sheep arrived from Australia. The sheep adapted well to New Zealand's rough, hilly landscape, and their wool provided the settlers with their first source of income. Large farm homes and great stations, or sheep ranches, were built on the strength of wool sales.

While the fortunes of the European immigrants improved, the Maoris' existence did not. With the arrival of the Pakehas, much of the Maoris' land was sold or taken away from them. What remained was often poor in quality and nearly impossible to farm successfully.

The Maoris felt confused by the Treaty of Waitangi. They could not understand how all these settlers had land that the Maoris thought belonged to the government. In 1845, this confusion led to a battle between the Maoris and the Pakehas.

The new governor, Sir George Grey, first used troops to stop the fighting, but soon he was able to win the trust of the Maoris. With Grey as governor, New Zealand experienced a period of order and progress. However, conditions still did not improve for the Maoris. Not only were they losing their land, but many of their people continued to die from diseases and alcohol brought by the Pakehas. The Maori population was declining at an alarming rate. From Captain Cook's arrival until 1858, it dropped from 200,000 to about 56,000. As the situation grew worse, the Maori people decided to put aside their tribal differences and band together. In 1858, an old Waikato leader named Te Wherowhero was elected to be the first Maori king. After his election, the people decided not to sell any more of their land.

The settlers, enjoying their first successes from the wool trade, saw this move as an act of rebellion. In 1860, British and colonial troops invaded the Maori lands. That invasion started a long period of fighting,

now called the Maori Wars, or Land Wars.

Over the next ten years, fighting on the North Island left the settlers economically drained and the Maori race nearly destroyed. By the time the settlers finally defeated the Maoris in 1870, 1,000 settlers and 2,000 Maoris had lost their lives. The government then punished the "rebels" by taking away even more of their land.

Gold, Refrigeration, and "King Dick"

Because very few Maoris lived on South Island, the land there was easier for pioneers to buy from the government. Away from the fighting on North Island, the fortunes of South Island's settlers improved during the 1860s. In 1861, a prospector named Gabriel Read discovered gold in Otago, which started a massive gold rush. Gold diggers from as far away as China and California came to New Zealand. Mining this valuable metal was important to New Zealand's economy for many years.

In 1882, the *Dunedin*, the first refrigerated ship to transport goods out of New Zealand, traveled to Britain with a load of mutton. Now, the nation had found another successful export besides gold and wool. Refrigeration meant that items such as meat, butter, and cheese could be shipped without spoiling. It helped

Sheep graze on New Zealand's hilly pastures. The colony's early European immigrants soon made profits in the wool trade.

establish the meat and dairy industries New Zealanders still rely on today.

During the 1880s, thousands of immigrants arrived in New Zealand. Too poor to buy farms, they often had to look for jobs in towns and factories. There they were forced to work long, unhealthy hours for little money. When the world prices for gold and wool dropped, many people lost their jobs.

Richard Seddon became prime minister in 1893. "King Dick," as Seddon was nicknamed, introduced changes in social policies. Under his leadership, New Zealand began its social-welfare programs such as old-age pensions and labor laws. Trade unions grew strong and worked for new laws that improved the immigrants' poor working conditions.

The Maori community experienced a renewal of its own. Maui Pomare, Apirana Turupa Ngata, and Peter Buck were leading members of the Young Maori Party, which helped to improve Maoris' education and health. Pomare, Ngata, and Buck traveled to Maori villages. They encouraged Maoris to make use of modern medicine to cure diseases, to keep their villages clean in order to prevent disease, and to eat better foods. Their efforts helped create a new era of Maori pride. It was an era, too, of survival and growing confidence. The population began to rebuild, in numbers, strength, and health, for the first time since the arrival of the white settlers.

The New Century

As the twentieth century dawned, New Zealand gained more independence from England. In 1907, the colony was granted dominion status, which meant that it was now a self-governing land. New Zealanders already had a reputation as an independent people who took strong stands on issues. In 1893, their government became the first in the world to give women the right to vote. In 1898, it was the first to set up a social security system.

New Zealand was growing stronger and more independent, but it still had problems. In 1915, Maori and Pakeha soldiers joined Australian troops to form the ANZACs, or Australian and New Zealand Corps. The ANZACs proved their bravery on Turkey's Gallipoli Peninsula, where they fought to take control of the Dardanelles, a narrow strait separating Europe and Turkey. In this campaign, which lasted from April to December 1915, thousands of ANZACs were killed.

During World War I, 50,000 soldiers from New Zealand were wounded and 17,000 died. The country, which had only one million people at that time, took many years to recover. In 1918, the year the war ended, a terrible flu swept through the country, killing many more New Zealanders, especially Maoris.

The next decade, too, was a difficult time, mainly for the nation's farmers. World prices for agricultural products began to drop. The Great Depression of the 1930s meant that British markets could no longer afford to buy New Zealand's exports. By 1933, many of the country's farmers had gone bankrupt. At least 100,000 people lost their jobs. Poverty and hopelessness spread throughout the small, remote nation.

The welfare reforms, a source of pride to New Zealanders, proved useless during these hard times. The government had no money to give out, and people were hungry. Riots in Auckland and Wellington expressed the citizens' frustration and despair. They demanded changes in their government.

A new system arrived with the election of 1935, and the victory of the Labour Party's Michael J. Savage. With Savage as prime minister, New Zealand improved and expanded its welfare system. The basic wage was raised, and low-rent houses were built. Pensions and medical aid were increased. Once more, New Zealand was recognized as a social leader.

When World War II was declared in 1939, New Zealand sent troops to aid the Allies against Germany, Italy, and Japan. In 1945, when the war ended, the country again had to recover from severe losses. More than 10,000 of New Zealand's soldiers had been killed.

After World War II, there were more jobs than workers because of the many soldiers lost in the war. The government attracted immigrants to rebuild the population by offering free travel fares and helping to find jobs for the newcomers.

In 1947, the British government signed the Statute of Westminster. Under this law, New Zealand became a completely independent nation.

One People

As New Zealand moves into the twenty-first century, it carries with it a new spirit of the Treaty of Waitangi. When the treaty was signed in 1840, Captain Hobson said to the assembled Maori leaders, "We are now one people." Since the nation's early days, its citizens have worked hard toward becoming one people, but it has not always been easy.

In the late 1980s, the New Zealand Court of Appeals examined the Treaty of Waitangi. The court redefined the treaty to express a "principle of partnership" between the races. Important Maori lands and fishing rights were returned to the native people, and the Maori language was recognized as an official language of New Zealand. New Zealanders hope that in the future this treaty will help to improve relations between New Zealand's native citizens and those who settled there later.

The government is working both to unite its citizens and to define its relationship with other countries. In the

David Lange served as prime minister from 1984 to 1989.

1980s, under the leadership of Prime Minister David Lange, New Zealand declared the nation a Nuclear Free Zone. This is an area where nuclear activities are banned. In 1985, New Zealand refused to allow in its ports any American navy vessels that would not declare if they were nuclear-powered or carrying nuclear weapons. As a result, New Zealand was no longer allowed to remain a member of ANZUS, an alliance for defense it had shared with Australia and the United States since 1951.

New Zealand's strong anti-nuclear policy led to trouble in Auckland Harbour on a July day in 1985. Attempting to prevent a protest against French nuclear testing in the South Pacific, French secret service agents bombed and sank the *Rainbow Warrior*. This ship belonged to Greenpeace, a group dedicated to protecting wildlife and the environment. A photographer was killed in the explosion.

On August 1, 1989, Prime Minister David Lange resigned. The Deputy Prime Minister, Geoffrey Palmer, took Lange's place until the next election. Within a day, Geoffrey Palmer announced that New Zealand would continue to ban American navy ships from its coastal waters because the ships might carry nuclear weapons.

This small nation remains strongly independent as it looks forward to the twenty-first century. Today, New Zealanders are united more than ever before. Working together, the people of this remote South Pacific country will continue to express their concerns in world affairs.

4. Maoritanga

Maoritanga means the Maori way of life. To modern Maoris, the word symbolizes a living heritage. To their ancestors, it meant a state of being where gods, people, and nature lived as a sacred whole. Maoritanga is stronger now than at any time since the arrival of the first Pakehas, or white people. Although most Maoris today live in a modern world filled with many European traditions, they work hard to keep their own language and traditions alive.

New Zealanders are proud of Maoritanga. Important officials who visit from other countries are greeted with a traditional Maori welcome, complete with singing and dancing. Maori words are a common part of conversation in New Zealand. Most of the country's citizens are familiar with Maori customs and stories. Many of these traditions date back to the days of the classic Maori culture.

"Tapu" Means Sacred

In classic Maori society, almost everyone in a tribe was related to each other. The leader was the most sacred, or *tapu*, figure in the tribe. Tapu to the Maoris still

A modern-day Maori girl dresses in the traditional clothing of her ancestors. New Zealand's Maori people hold proudly to their rich cultural heritage.

means "sacred," but in the past it ruled every course of behavior from birth to death. A leader's body—especially his head—was sacred from the time he was born and could not be touched by ordinary people. Anything he touched or ate from immediately became tapu and off-limits to others.

The leader was also made special by his *mana*—his spiritual power or prestige. Gods were made of pure mana. In the world of human beings, a leader had the most mana. If he proved himself to be a brave and successful warrior, his mana increased. If he did something wrong or showed a weakness, his mana would quickly fade, and the entire tribe would be embarrassed.

The daily activities of Maori men and women were ruled by tapu. The men built houses and canoes, tended the fields, led fishing and hunting parties, and fought in battle as the tribe's warriors. The women made clothes, prepared food, and—most important for the future of the tribe—raised the children.

Normally, Maoris slept in single-room houses which had not been decorated because they were used only for sleeping. Maoris never cooked or ate food indoors. Cooked food was highly tapu, or sacred, and if it was brought inside, the building would have to be burned down. People took care never to eat inside a meeting-house, since the carved decorations could take years to complete.

A Maori meetinghouse.

Growing Up and Learning Tapu

Maori children led a carefree, easy life and were not disciplined or punished, no matter how badly they behaved. Parents thought that confident, independent children would make good warriors when they grew up.

Often, children helped with chores, perhaps by gathering firewood or learning to make baskets. Older girls took care of their younger brothers and sisters. Yet most of the time, the children played. Boys would play fighting games with mock weapons, in preparation for their future as warriors. Girls learned the songs and dances they would perform as adults. Twirling and spinning *poi* balls, tightly bound balls attached to long cords, taught the girls quickness and a sense of graceful rhythm.

A son of a leader could be an apprentice to a priest. A priest was often also an expert in a field such as carving or tattooing. It was common for a Maori man or woman to have a facial tattoo, known as a *moko*. A moko was as individual as a signature. In fact, many leaders drew their mokos as a signature when they signed the Treaty of Waitangi. A woman's moko covered only her lips and chin, but a man had his entire face tattooed. The process was very painful since a little chisel was used to carve the design into the skin. Even the bravest warriors could stand to be tattooed only for short periods of time, and a full moko could take many years to complete.

Study with a priest lasted for several years. At the end, the boys were tested with difficult examinations. They had to prove they had correctly memorized their lessons and had a complete knowledge of tapu.

Maori Stories

Maori adults were always willing to tell the children stories. Maui was a popular story character who had many funny and dangerous adventures, such as the time

This moko is painted on a modern-day Maori man. True mokos of the past—permanent tattoos carved into the skin—were much more painful to achieve.

he brought fire to humans from the fingernails of the fire goddess. One favorite story tells how Maui gave people enough time to work during the day.

Before Maui, the days were very short. The sun raced across the sky, and people never had time to do anything worthwhile. Maui thought that if he could catch the sun with flax ropes, he could make it slow down. But every time Maui tried, the heat of the sun burned the ropes to cinders. Finally, Maui made a rope from the hair of his sister, Ina, and he was able to catch the sun. Maui beat the sun until it promised to cross the sky more slowly.

Another story about Maui tells how he fished the entire North Island out of the ocean using his grandmother's jaw for a fishhook. Other Maori stories told to children might be about water monsters such as the *taniwha.*

Some stories involved ordinary people, rather than gods, goddesses, or monsters. A favorite features Hinemoa, the oldest daughter of the leader of a tribe. During her early life, Hinemoa was spoiled and pampered, but when she grew up, she was expected to marry the man her parents chose for her. Hinemoa did not agree. She decided not to marry any man picked by her parents.

Hinemoa lived beside Lake Rotorua. The man she wanted to marry, Tutanekai, lived on an island in the middle of the lake. Every night, Tutanekai played flute music to Hinemoa, and every night, Hinemoa's family pulled their canoes onto the shore to keep her from rowing over to Tutanekai. One night, Hinemoa could stand the separation no longer. She decided to swim the distance to Tutanekai. To keep herself afloat, she tied six empty gourds to her body and then struck out into the dark water.

After swimming for a long time, Hinemoa arrived on the island, exhausted, cold, and shivering. A nearby hot pool offered welcome relief, and Hinemoa sank down into its warmth to rest. Tutanekai, unaware that Hinemoa was on the island, sent a slave out to fetch some water. The slave came to the pool where Hinemoa huddled. As he dipped in his gourd, Hinemoa grabbed it and broke it, frightening the slave. The poor slave returned to his master for another gourd. But again the same thing happened, and yet again! Very angry, Tutanekai himself went to the pool where, to his astonishment and delight, he found Hinemoa. They were married and today are remembered in stories, songs, and even street names.

The Maori people of New Zealand believe an ancient explorer named Kupe was the first person to discover their beautiful island home. This is another story that has been told for generations.

More than 1,000 years ago, they say, Kupe set out from a legendary land called Hawaiiki. With his friends and family, Kupe crossed the South Pacific Ocean in canoes, searching for new territory. After a long, difficult voyage filled with fear, hunger, and thirst, Kupe's wife suddenly saw what she thought was a cloud. *"He ao! He ao!* (A cloud! A cloud!)" she cried. Kupe sailed nearer to the sight and gratefully realized the cloud was land. "Aotearoa," he called it, "Land of the Long White Cloud." Many Maoris still call their homeland Aotearoa instead of New Zealand.

Maoritanga Today

Today, many government and private programs work to keep Maoritanga alive. The Maori Arts and Crafts Institute in Rotorua teaches people traditional arts such as carving, weaving, and dancing.

The Maoris of classic Maori culture expressed their love of beauty in many forms besides their famous carvings. The fibers of the New Zealand flax plant, for instance, were woven into beautiful cloaks, which were decorated with kiwi or parrot feathers. Such cloaks often became prized family heirlooms. Tribal leaders dressed in dog-skin cloaks with the feathers of the *huia* bird in their hair. Both men and women wore greenstone pendants as necklaces and earrings. Maoris today believe that as long as these and their many other crafts and skills are remembered and passed on, the link between the present and their ancestors will remain unbroken.

But there is more to Maoritanga than just remembering the past. New songs, dances, stories, and customs continue to be created and will be taught to future generations. At the heart of all this activity is the *marae*, a large, open space outside the village meetinghouse. The meetinghouse—carved in great detail and named for a tribal ancestor—was the most important building in the classic Maori village. It served as the site of many social and religious activities.

A modern-day Maori dancer twirls poi balls.

The marae is still the center of Maori social life. It is the site of weddings, funerals, and all events of importance to the community. Today, a marae complex includes the sacred courtyard, the meetinghouse—still beautifully carved and named for an ancestor—and any other special building, such as a church. When people visit a marae, they must follow certain rules in order not to break tapu. Visitors must dress nicely and show respect for their surroundings and each other. No one is allowed to speak or walk around until the elders have completed a formal welcoming ceremony.

There are now more than 800 marae throughout New Zealand. All of them teach the values of family and hospitality. Many marae are located in towns and suburbs, making it easier for all New Zealanders to share in this rich and growing culture.

5. Upside-Down Holidays

In New Zealand, almost every day of the year is marked by a special festival, show, or celebration somewhere in the country. Special events range from the International Festival of the Arts to the fun of nonsense celebrations. One such holiday, Gumboot Day, features a contest in which gumboots, or rainboots, are thrown for distance.

What might make New Zealand holidays seem confusing to North Americans are the backward seasons—everything seems reversed. Christmas takes place during summer vacation, and Easter usually has a harvest theme!

In New Zealand, working people get nine legal holidays throughout the year, plus at least three weeks of paid vacation. New Zealanders value their free time. They believe that everyone should enjoy weekends and holidays with leisure rather than work.

Springtime

Spring in New Zealand is lambing season. In a country with 60 million sheep, you can imagine the number of lambs born every year! Children often keep lambs as pets, and even the public parks devote some

Two young New Zealanders play with their pet lambs.

small area to grazing. In Auckland, it is almost a spring-time tradition to walk through the fields of daffodils in Cornwall Park and watch the lambs frisking in the sun.

The first real spring holiday is Labour Day, celebrated on the fourth Monday of October. Workers and schoolchildren have this day off. Weather permitting, it is marked by the first swim of the year.

Spring's most exciting holiday for children is Guy Fawkes Day on November 5. Guy Fawkes Day has its

origins in English history and the story of the Gunpow-
der Plot, an unsuccessful plan to blow up the English
Parliament and King James I in 1605. Guy Fawkes, one
of the traitors, was caught and hung. Today, New Zealand children follow English tradition by using old
clothes and rags to make a figure which they call the
"Guy." On Guy Fawkes night, they get together for
bonfire parties. When the wood for the bonfire is ready,
the Guy is placed on top. The fire is then started, the
Guy is consumed in the flames, and fireworks and spar-
klers are set off. As the fire burns down, the embers are
put to good use for roasting sausages.

A Summer Christmas

After Guy Fawkes Day, New Zealand's children
eagerly wait for summer vacation and Christmas. Every
year, someone writes to the newspapers to suggest that
New Zealand celebrate Christmas in July, when the
weather in the country is more wintry. But this idea has
never met with any official success.

The first signs of Christmas are the *pohutakawa*
trees in bloom. These twisted trees, native to New Zealand, line many North Island beaches. At Christmastime, they burst into brilliant red flowers.

During the Christmas season, many families leave
town for their summer vacations. In late December and

A pohutakawa tree in full bloom on the Coromandel Peninsula at Christmastime.

early January, most of the islands' people can be found at a campground or by the shore. Some families own small holiday homes, called "bachs" (pronounced BATCH·uhz) in the North Island and "cribs" in the South Island. Bachs and cribs are very informal, frequently furnished with odd, unwanted tables, chairs, and other pieces from home. Here, families can relax, and nobody gets into trouble for tracking sand inside the house!

Whether they choose to travel or stay at home,

Like thousands of New Zealanders, these three young beach-combers happily spend their Christmas vacation by the shore.

New Zealanders put up a small Christmas tree—perhaps one they have cut for themselves. Children wait for Santa Claus, or Father Christmas, as he is often called. Presents are opened on Christmas morning, after which people might visit friends. Despite the warm temperatures, a roast lamb or turkey dinner is served in the middle of the day.

Christmas wouldn't be Christmas without crackers, paper party favors that make a popping noise when the ends are pulled apart. Crackers are opened before dinner so that the funny hats inside can be worn during the meal. No holiday meal is complete without plum pudding or trifle—a dessert of cake, custard, and fruit—followed by fruitcake. New Zealand's fruitcake is more like a raisin cake. For Christmas, it is covered with a thick layer of almond paste and topped with a hard, sugary icing. The cake is then surrounded with frilly, bright paper and decorated with tiny Christmas ornaments such as reindeer and snowmen.

Christmas Day is followed by Boxing Day, an English holiday, on December 26. On Boxing Day, New Zealanders give a Christmas box or a present of money to the newspaper carrier, milk delivery person, or anyone else who has given them good service throughout the year. Most people use the day to sleep off their Christmas dinner.

New Year's Day is another summer holiday, and New Zealanders often take January 2 off as well. In January, Auckland and Wellington celebrate their anniversary days; other cities and regions hold their anniversary festivities at different times of the year. Auckland's Anniversary Day, January 29, is always celebrated with a splendid yachting race in the harbor. Anything that floats takes part in the event, from huge, luxurious yachts to home-built rowboats.

The last holiday of the summer is Waitangi Day on February 6. On this day, people gather in many places throughout the country to re-enact the signing of the

Treaty of Waitangi. Participants dress in nineteenth-century costumes, with some people acting the parts of Captain Hobson and the Maori leaders. But because the treaty has brought the Maoris so much unhappiness, many New Zealanders believe that it is wrong to celebrate. Protestors sometimes clash with the police outside the ceremonies, which has made the holiday less popular than in the past. Now, some people simply call it New Zealand Day. Many New Zealanders wonder why the Treaty of Waitangi should be considered their nation's birthday, but a better date has yet to be chosen.

Autumn Festivals

Many festivals that hold excitement for New Zealanders take place during the autumn. The first, the River Regatta, is held at Ngaruawahia, a town near Hamilton. It is a Maori festival that dates back to the beginning of the twentieth century. Tourists from around the world come to watch this famous event. Decorated Maori war canoes are launched down the Waikato River in an impressive display of rowing and boat-racing contests. The River Regatta also gives Maori tribes the opportunity to compete against each other in traditional skills such as poi twirling.

Scottish traditions come alive at another major event of the fall season, the Hastings Highlands Games. Besides

Splendidly decorated Maori war canoes parade down the Wai-kato River in the River Regatta at Ngaruawahia.

the bagpipe bands and Highland dancing, *haggis* throwing attracts a lot of attention. Haggis is a Scottish meal of oatmeal-stuffed sheeps' stomachs. According to legend, in the village where haggis was first made, the women used to throw it to their husbands across the river for lunch. At the Highlands Games, the haggis is thrown for fun and competition.

Easter is another holiday New Zealanders turn into a long weekend—Good Friday and the Monday after

Easter are both public holidays. Easter is a quieter holiday than Christmas, and children may go to church with their families and spend some of the day hunting for chocolate Easter eggs. On the extra days off, people often travel to the Easter festivals and shows sponsored by different cities. During these festivals, schoolchildren take part in precision marching, dance competitions, and horse-riding events. Special displays feature their prize-winning vegetables, artwork, knitting, cooking, and pet animals. Young people especially enjoy the fairground games and rides that are always part of the Easter shows.

An important fall holiday is ANZAC Day, April 25, a day to remember all those who have given their lives in war. The day takes its name from the soldiers in the Australian and New Zealand Corps who served so bravely in World War I. Today, ANZAC Day honors New Zealanders who lost their lives in all wars. It is observed with memorial services and veterans' parades, and is a time for young and old alike to reflect quietly on the consequences of war.

Winter Shows

The Queen's Birthday on the first Monday in June announces the beginning of winter. Queen Elizabeth's real birthday is April 21, but the official celebration was changed to June so that her subjects in England could have a warmer, more pleasant summer holiday. Because New Zealand lies in the Southern Hemisphere, the change meant a colder holiday. Today, the Queen's Birthday often marks the opening of the snow-ski season.

Winter is also the time for the world-famous New Zealand Agricultural Field Days, held at Mystery Creek near Hamilton. Although Mystery Creek's Field Days are among the best known, more than eighty agricultural shows are held throughout the country every year. Agricultural shows are similar to American state fairs— farmers and their families attend the shows to inspect the best of New Zealand's livestock and the latest labor-saving inventions. What they learn at the show can prepare them for yet another year of spring lambs and autumn harvests.

6. A Taste of New Zealand

Exported food products are a major part of New Zealand's economy. New Zealanders have high standards for the taste and appearance of their foods. The country's dairy products are especially creamy, its fruits are extra juicy, and its meat and fish are among the finest in the world. Perhaps this is why many people in this nation eat close to six meals a day!

Home Cooking and Takeaways

New Zealanders like to start the day with a full breakfast, such as eggs, sausages, and bacon. A few hours after breakfast, they enjoy a snack called morning tea. Tea shops do a thriving business between 10:00 and 11:00 A.M. as customers eat sausage rolls, or sausages wrapped in pastry, and cream-filled doughnuts washed down by several cups of tea.

Lunch is usually an informal meal made up of foods such as hand-held meat pies filled with minced steak, sometimes with a top crust of mashed potatoes. Hamburgers are another lunch food. But in a country where the people prefer their food fresh, mass-produced fast foods are not very popular. Instead, customers

A New Zealand afternoon tea, with plenty of cakes and cream.

prefer to order a hefty meat patty layered with a fried egg, plenty of real cheese, lettuce, and sliced beets and tomatoes in a fresh bread roll. A New Zealand burger may take a little longer to prepare, but it is worth waiting for.

New Zealanders tend to be friendly people who enjoy entertaining. Afternoon tea is a good opportunity for them to visit and show their baking skills at the same time. Scones, a heavier version of American biscuits, are served with whipped cream and jam. Other standard teatime treats include fruit cakes, custard squares and shortbread.

Dinner may also be called "tea" in New Zealand, which can create confusing situations. Dinner guests expected in the evening sometimes show up in the afternoon! Roast lamb with mint sauce is the dinner traditionally prepared for guests. It is served with roast potatoes, roast *kumara*—the New Zealand sweet potato—and roast pumpkin. New Zealanders eat pumpkin as a vegetable, particularly in the winter when it is difficult to buy fresh greens.

For dessert, people might have apple pie and cream, or the national favorite, pavlova. Pavlova is a fluffy meringue covered in whipped cream and fruit. It was first created in the 1920s to celebrate the visit to New Zealand of the famous Russian ballerina, Anna Pavlova.

New Zealanders who are too busy to cook dinner might make a trip to the local fish'n'chips shop for some "takeaways." Deep-fried fish and thickly cut french fries wrapped in newspaper are among the most popular of New Zealand's specialties. At the takeaway shop, customers can also order milk shakes and ice-cream cones. New Zealand's ice cream is flavored with big chunks of fruit, and most people want double scoops of it in their milk shakes.

Just before going to bed, New Zealanders often have a hot drink and another little pastry or toast spread with Marmite, a thick beef and yeast spread. This late-night snack is called supper. At this time children usually have Milo, a chocolaty drink with vitamins.

Cooking the New Zealand Way

Many of New Zealand's foods and eating habits—such as afternoon tea and cream cakes—come from England. In recent years, the large number of Pacific Island immigrants have also introduced their ethnic foods to the country. Taro, a starchy root vegetable eaten in the islands, is now sold in most Auckland vegetable shops. Island recipes such as fish cooked in coconut milk with pineapple have become tasty additions in many New Zealand kitchens.

The Maoris were the first people to fish the country's coastline for its famous oysters, mussels, and clams. *Pipis* are a type of clam that children in particular enjoy. A full bucket of pipis steamed open over a fire and then sprinkled with vinegar and eaten on slices of buttered bread is a true New Zealand beach lunch.

Another type of clam, the *toheroa*, can be found mainly at Northland's Ninety Mile Beach. Larger than pipis and much rarer, toheroas are made into a rich, dark-green soup New Zealanders would eat every day if they could. To keep toheroas from becoming extinct, the government has to control the number taken from the beach every year.

People from all over the world enjoy New Zealand's kiwi fruit in desserts, salads, and drinks. Other fruits, such as egg-shaped feijoas, tamarillos, and passion fruit, are not as familiar to overseas shoppers. Tamarillos have a tart, refreshing flavor, while passion fruit tastes like a smooth mixture of bananas, melons, and peaches. Feijoas are green inside like kiwi fruit, but with the flavor of bubble gum. They all taste good on ice cream.

With such a variety of foods, it is only natural that many New Zealanders have become gourmet cooks. Restaurants throughout the country compete with each other to create unusual, tempting recipes with local products. But for this nation's people, nothing compares with home cooking or a traditional Maori *hangi*.

A tempting fruit and vegetable stand in Auckland.

A hangi is a pit that the Maoris dig in the earth and use as an oven to cook meats and vegetables. In the past, most Maori meals were cooked in a hangi. Today, when New Zealanders say they are building a hangi, it usually means they are having a party where the food will be cooked in this traditional way.

Building a hangi requires a group effort. First, a deep pit is dug in the ground, and a wood fire is lighted on the floor of the pit. Stones are placed on top of the

New Zealanders dish up steamed lamb and kumaras at a traditional Maori hangi.

flames. As the wood burns, the red-hot stones fall to the bottom. After the flames die out, a layer of leaves and fern fronds goes on next, followed by the food. Lamb, pork chops, potatoes, and kumaras—New Zealand sweet potatoes—are wrapped in leaves or aluminum foil, and placed on the fern fronds. A final layer of leaves is placed on top of the food, weighted down by more hot stones. Water is generously sprinkled over everything before placing flax mats on top and covering the pit with soil. The food then steams for several hours and comes out cooked to perfection.

More Delicious Dishes

A hangi is a lot of fun, but you might find it easier to try a taste of New Zealand by making a few simpler dishes. Here are some typical New Zealand recipes that aren't too difficult to prepare.

Samoan Baked Fish

2 pounds mildly flavored white fish, such as cod or
  halibut
1 tablespoon salt
1-1/2 cups canned coconut milk

Wash the fish and rub it with the salt. Place the salted fish in a baking dish. Pour one cup of coconut milk over the fish. Bake in a 350-degree oven for one hour, or until fish is tender. (After forty minutes, check to see if fish is drying out. If so, add one-half cup more coconut milk.) Serve with rice, sliced pineapple, and a crisp, green salad. Serves four.

Super Pumpkin Soup

2 pounds, or 1 kilogram, pumpkin (if pumpkin is not available, try substituting acorn or butternut squash)

2 large onions
1/2 teaspoon salt
1/2 teaspoon pepper
water
2-1/2 cups milk
2 tablespoons butter
grated cheese
chopped parsley
buttered whole-grain toast

Wash the pumpkin, peel or scrape it if desired, and cut it into small pieces. Chop the onions coarsely. Put the pumpkin, onions, salt, and pepper in a large saucepan with enough water to cover the mixture. Bring the water to a boil, and simmer until the pumpkin is tender. When it is tender, drain off all the water, saving about one cup of the liquid.

Mash the pumpkin, and add the milk and some of the pumpkin water until the soup is as thick or as thin as you like. Reheat, and stir in the butter, with added salt and pepper to taste. Remove from the heat before the soup boils. Ladle it into soup bowls, sprinkle with cheese and parsley, and serve with buttered whole-grain toast. Serves four.

Kiwi Fruit Smoothie Drink

cracked ice
kiwi fruit
vanilla ice cream

For each serving, put one cup of cracked ice, two peeled kiwi fruit, and one scoop of vanilla ice cream into a blender. Blend for several seconds or until smooth, and then pour into a tall glass.

Pikelets, which are like small pancakes, are a favorite with New Zealand children for dessert or afternoon tea. Because pikelets are eaten cold, they can be made ahead of time.

Pikelets

1 egg
1/4 cup sugar
1 cup sifted flour
1/4 teaspoon salt
1 teaspoon baking powder
3/4 cup milk
1 teaspoon melted butter
butter, raspberry jam, and whipped cream

Beat the egg and sugar together until the mixture is thick. In another bowl, mix the sifted flour, salt, and baking powder. Stir the milk into the egg and sugar mixture, and then add all three to the flour mixture. Next, add the melted butter, and stir until it is smooth. Cook in spoonfuls on a hot, greased frying pan or griddle. Let the pikelets cool to room temperature, and serve them with butter, raspberry or other fruit jam, and whipped cream. Serves four.

7. A Good Education for All

During most of the nineteenth century, obtaining an education in New Zealand was not easy. Unless they were wealthy, most immigrant and Maori children learned only as much as their parents or missionaries could teach them. The Education Act of 1877 changed this situation. It required children to go to school and established the first free public schools.

In the years immediately following the act, several teachers' training colleges were opened. The Sumner Institute, the world's first government-funded school for the deaf, was founded. These early efforts toward better education were soon joined by art schools, schools for the blind, and schools for the mentally handicapped.

Today, school is required for young people between the ages of six and fifteen, and many children begin their education even earlier. Most of New Zealand's schools are run by the government. Only 3 percent of all students attend private or religious schools. In New Zealand, private schools can choose to be part of the public, state-sponsored system. By following the state guidelines for courses of study, they receive free textbooks and funds to help maintain buildings and pay teachers' salaries.

Some farm children in isolated areas of New Zealand do not go to school. They receive homework from their teachers in the mail.

The government also provides the national Correspondence School for children who live in isolated areas. Teachers at the Correspondence School in Wellington send books and lessons to their students through the mail. After the children complete their assignments, they put them in an envelope and mail them back to their teachers.

The New Zealand school year consists of three terms. The first school term begins in February and lasts until May, when the children take a two-week holiday. The second term runs from June until mid-August, followed by another two weeks of vacation. The third term lasts from September until early December, when the schools take a six- or seven-week break. High school students take an extra week without classes in August to study for their exams.

Preschool

Preschools in New Zealand are designed to teach children that learning and sharing can be fun. While some preschools are private, most receive funding from the government. Playgroups welcome babies as young as a few weeks old, and two-year-olds can attend playcenters until they turn five. By the time they are three years of age, children may attend state-run kindergartens.

Te Kohanga Reo, a type of preschool found only in New Zealand, offers a new approach to learning. In Maori, te Kohanga Reo means "the language nests." In language nests, preschool Maori and other children learn the Maori language, culture, and values in a completely Maori-speaking environment. Maori elders started the first language nest in 1982. By the end of that year, at least fifty of these preschools were in operation across the country.

Preschool children play counting games at a te Kohanga Reo school.

Supporters of te Kohanga Reo hope that the next generation of New Zealanders will be able to speak both English and Maori. Across the country today, 450 language nests are teaching children the Maori language before they enter school.

Take Out Your Exercise Books

Most of New Zealand's children enter primary school on the day after their fifth birthday. If their birthdays occur during, or close to, one of the long school vacations, they wait until the new term to join the class. Children spend the first two years of primary school in the "infant classes" before they begin the standards. Standards 1 through 4 are similar to the American third through sixth grades. Children are usually seven years old in Standard 1 and about ten years old by the time they reach Standard 4.

The primary-school day runs from 9:00 A.M. to 3:00 P.M. A typical day in a Standard 3 or 4 class starts with a lesson on the recorder, a simple wind instrument like a flute. After mastering their new piece of music, the students may practice their handwriting or spelling. Usually they write in bound notebooks called exercise books. Math follows handwriting, and then the students are given a fifteen-minute recess outside. After recess, they may return to their math lesson before moving on to reading. Some days, the children read silently to themselves or work on a computer. Once a week, they go to the school library to check out books or read copies of the *School Journal*, a magazine published for New Zealand's schools since 1907.

Afternoon classes include less structured lessons such as art. Sports finish the afternoon. The schoolchildren rush outside to play cricket, soccer, softball, hockey, or rugby before going home. Because New Zealand is surrounded by beaches, many primary schools include swimming and water-safety lessons in swimming

Primary school students take a field trip to the Museum of Transport and Technology in Auckland.

pools as part of the school day. Several times a year, schoolchildren also take field trips to museums, state parks, and zoos.

Intermediate and High School

The standards are followed by intermediate school, which is similar to junior high school in the United States. Intermediate school is divided into Forms 1 and

2, similar to the seventh and eighth grades. After intermediate school, New Zealand's young people begin high school—or "college," as it is sometimes called—which consists of Forms 3 through 7. High school students attend classes from 8:45 A.M. to 3:15 P.M.

Boys and girls often attend separate high schools in New Zealand. Many private schools and schools in the cities are open to only boys or girls. Both private and public high school students are usually required to wear uniforms. New Zealanders believe uniforms promote a feeling of equality among the students—no one can ever feel "in" or "out" just because of the clothes he or she wears. Yet teenagers may dislike wearing uniforms and sometimes compete with each other to see whose uniform can look the worst. Because uniforms are expensive, schools and parents discourage such behavior.

One way parents can afford to pay for school uniforms is to use their family benefit. This is a weekly allowance that the government pays to families for each child. The benefit is paid from the time children are born until they are fifteen or, if they stay in school, until they are eighteen. Parents can choose to receive the money in a lump sum each year to help with the cost of uniforms, school shoes, and other needed supplies.

High school students usually take a total of six subjects during the school year. Until they are in the sixth form, all students must study mathematics and English.

Intermediate and high school students at the private Christ's College in Christchurch have finished their classes for the day.

For their remaining courses, they may choose from history, geography, Maori studies, a foreign language such as French or Russian, science, accounting, technical drawing, art, and music. Both boys and girls may take physical education, workshop crafts, or home economics. In the sixth and seventh forms, students may choose all of their classes.

To some students, these subjects seem pointless. They would rather leave school and get a job as soon as they turn fifteen. Those who continue with school often decide the sixth form is enough. After completing Form 6, they are given the Sixth Form Certificate, which shows they have finished four years of high school.

University Study

Students who plan to attend one of New Zealand's six universities sometimes take an extra year of high school, called the seventh form. Seventh form students take special university scholarship exams at the end of the year. The extra year also helps prepare students for university work, since a bachelor's degree in New Zealand is an intense three-year course of study.

Although New Zealand's six universities are located in different major cities on the two main islands, they are all part of the state-sponsored system and offer the same general courses of study. Some universities specialize in certain fields, though, such as medicine, agriculture, or teacher training. University education is free. Full-time university students are paid an allowance to help them afford rent, food, and textbooks.

Continuing Education

Fifteen is an early age to leave school and try to find a job. It is a choice many New Zealanders make but sometimes regret. "School leavers" are not dropouts in the American sense, but their limited education can soon lead to unemployment. Fortunately, a hasty decision to leave school can be reversed. People can return to their studies at any time and even receive financial support from the government to achieve their goals.

New Zealand's government is trying to encourage students to remain in school. As the nation's industry and agriculture move toward a future in which technology plays a larger role, a well-educated population will be vital to the country's growth. Although education is important to everyone around the world, in New Zealand the situation is at a turning point. If New Zealand is to remain an independent part of the world's economy, its young people must be convinced to continue their education. Otherwise, the nation may find itself depending on the technologies of other countries, with nothing of its own to trade in return.

8. The Sporting Life

New Zealanders are often pictured as sports fanatics, spending their spare moments kicking rugby balls or racing on snow skis. Many of the country's athletes hope to represent New Zealand at the Olympic Games. Considering its small population, New Zealand has produced a high number of Olympic medal winners over the years.

Sports and recreation play important roles in the people's lives. But of greatest interest to most New Zealanders are family fun and good sporting attitudes.

Rugby and Cricket

If one sport had to be chosen as New Zealand's national game, it would likely be rugby, a relative of American football. Many local and regional rugby teams compete in New Zealand, but the national rugby team, the *All Blacks*, is world-famous. This name comes from the players' black shorts and shirts. Every year, the All Blacks represent New Zealand by playing against national teams from other countries, either at home or abroad.

Rugby matches are fast-paced, rough, muddy

Rugby fans cheer for the All Blacks during a match in New Zealand.

games. The players do not wear helmets or any sort of padding, and yet they may tackle their opponents. If a player is injured, no substitutions are allowed.

Cricket, a team sport that draws almost as much attention as rugby, is known for its good manners. An expression heard often in New Zealand is "That's not cricket," meaning that a person's behavior is not fair or sporting. Although New Zealand has a professional national cricket team, it is common in the summertime to see informal cricket games in local parks. Spectators drink tea under the trees while cricket players in their white shirts, sweaters, and trousers play a game that can take hours or days to complete.

Cricket is played with a bat and ball by two teams of eleven players each. The teams try to defend their wickets, three upright wooden sticks placed in a row at both ends of the field. Balancing on top of each set of wickets are two small, delicate pieces of wood called "bails." Bowlers, who are like baseball pitchers, try to knock over the opposing team's bails, which are defended by a batsman.

Racetrack Fans

For some New Zealanders, the idea of an all-day cricket match holds less appeal. Instead, they seek excitement and action at the racetrack. There, they may

A morning exercise run at a racetrack.

cheer on racehorses, race-car drivers, or runners.

Horse racing has long been popular in New Zealand. One famous horse born in New Zealand was Phar Lap, the winner of the 1930 Melbourne Cup in Australia. This champion's life story was made into a movie.

Families that raise horses often participate in weekend show-jumping events. One New Zealander who started competing this way, Mark Todd, has been riding since he was seven years old. In both 1984 and 1988, he won gold medals for the Olympic equestrian three-day event.

Automobile and motorcycle racing also draw huge crowds in New Zealand, as do speedway and motocross events. During the 1960s, Bruce McClaren and Denis Hulme brought fame and recognition to the country by winning many Formula One events. In 1967, Hulme's victories led him to win the Formula One world championship—the highest and most famous award of car racing's top series.

Running is another field in which New Zealanders have excelled. Olympic gold medals in track and field were awarded to Jack Lovelock in 1936, Murray Halberg in 1960, Peter Snell in 1960 and 1964, and John Walker in 1976.

Marathon running is especially popular in New Zealand. About 80,000 runners take part in Auckland's Round the Bays race every March. Allison Roe became an international star in the early 1980s. In 1981, she came in first in the women's division of the Auckland marathon. That year Roe also won marathons in Japan, Boston, Atlanta, Sydney, and New York, where she set a new world record of 2 hours, 25 minutes, and 28 seconds.

A World of Water Sports

Sailing around New Zealand's bays can be as thrilling as a marathon race. Auckland's yacht owners—or

A family sails on the Bay of Islands.

"yachties," as they are called—have a wide choice of sailing destinations. The fifty small, forested islands of the Hauraki Gulf Maritime Park outside Auckland are perfect for a day's outing. Families can set sail in the morning for an island picnic and swim, and be back in their marina before dark.

Throughout the world, New Zealanders compete in yacht races. Bruce Kendall won an Olympic gold medal in 1988 for yacht racing. Other New Zealanders have sailed in the America's Cup race, the most famous sailboat competition in the world. When the United States won the cup in 1987, New Zealander Michael Fay challenged the Americans to an immediate rematch, instead of waiting the traditional three years. Fay lost the race, but in 1989 he was awarded the cup when he took the U.S. team to court over its choice of boat. Today, however, the courts are still debating which country deserves the cup.

Jetboating is another New Zealand water sport for adventurers. The high-powered jetboats are designed for the country's short, fast-flowing inland waters. Jetboats speed passengers down river shallows, passing close to rocky shores and bumping through narrow gorges. These same white waters are excellent for canoeing and kayaking—a sport that produced Olympic gold medals for New Zealanders Ian Ferguson and Paul McDonald in 1988.

Snow-skiing and Outdoor Safety

Snow-skiing is very popular with New Zealanders. Both the North and South islands have ski slopes with a full range of tow bars and chair lifts. The snow-ski season lasts from the end of June until late October. Sometimes schools take special ski trips during the August school holidays. To save money, people often join ski clubs that own and maintain lodges or huts in the mountains.

Young New Zealanders learn to snowplow in the Southern Alps.

During the summer when the snow melts, the ski slopes become some of New Zealand's most scenic hiking areas. The government established a network of trails, called "walkways," that are graded by their degree of difficulty.

Hikers, skiers, and mountain climbers must be aware of New Zealand's sometimes dangerous weather. Pleasant weather can quickly change into cold, rainy, and dangerous conditions without warning. Outward Bound courses at Queen Charlotte Sound in the South Island teach people the safest ways to use and enjoy the changeable environment. By experiencing situations that at first may be unfamiliar and even frightening—such as mountain climbing or river rafting—participants learn self-confidence and survival skills.

New Zealand's government supports many outdoor programs and activities. New Zealanders believe that sports and recreation are important ways of bringing people closer together while improving the quality of their daily life.

9. Globe-Trotting New Zealanders

Despite New Zealand's appealing scenery, food, recreation, and social-welfare system, thousands of its citizens decide to leave the country every year. In 1986, more than 57,000 emigrants left the islands to move to Australia and Europe. In 1987, another 58,000 New Zealanders moved to other countries. A small percentage of emigrants come to the United States to work or study, but most prefer Australia and England because of family ties and the similar cultures.

One reason people leave New Zealand is its size. The country is so small that it cannot support large numbers of professional people. Many New Zealanders who have the skills to be architects, journalists, fashion designers, and inventors find that the positions they want are already filled. Some people with a good business sense experience different problems. High manufacturing and shipping costs often prevent new or unusual ideas from going into production.

Young New Zealanders who are talented in the creative arts may run into other difficulties. With few other people to compete against, many young artists, singers, dancers, actors, and writers gain fame too quickly, with little real satisfaction. When it is too easy to become famous locally, they may feel the need to test their talents against the world's best.

Such frustrating situations may lead qualified New Zealanders to feel they have only two choices—to remain at home or to seek challenging and fulfilling positions in other countries. This is not a recent trend. In the early 1900s, the writer Katherine Mansfield, the painter Frances Hodgkins, and the first man to split the atom, Sir Ernest Rutherford, left New Zealand. They needed to find creative opportunities and recognition that their own small society could not offer.

Even people who believe they have everything they want in New Zealand sometimes feel the need to spend at least a few years abroad. Living so far from the rest of the world can give some New Zealanders a sense of being cut off from other cultures. Travel allows them to see the great museums and historical sites they have read about.

Travel Brings Fame and Reward

To help talented New Zealanders reach their artistic goals, the government's Queen Elizabeth II Arts Council awards grants. Sometimes the award money can be used to study overseas. One person who received such a grant and went on to become an international success is the Maori opera star Dame Kiri Te Kanawa.

New Zealand's world famous opera star, Dame Kiri Te Kanawa.

Originally from the town of Gisborne in the North Island, Kiri Te Kanawa is famous today for her singing voice and acting abilities. At the age of twenty-two, Kiri—whose name means "bell" in Maori—used her grant from the arts council to study in London. Five years later, in 1971, she signed her first contract to sing at one of the world's greatest opera houses, the Royal Opera House in London's Covent Garden.

Kiri was asked to sing at the 1981 wedding of

Britain's Prince Charles and Lady Diana Spencer. Besides singing for the royal couple's guests in London's Saint Paul's Cathedral, Kiri entertained more than 600 million people who were watching the wedding on television.

During Kiri's career, thousands of fans have enjoyed her performances in operas such as *Cosi Fan Tutti, The Magic Flute, La Traviata, Marriage of Figaro,* and *Don Giovanni.* Today, Kiri's performances are often shown on television, giving thousands of people the pleasure of watching her in concert.

Traveling for Adventure

While some New Zealanders go abroad to enrich their education and careers, others travel in search of adventure. Sir Edmund Hillary is best known to Americans for his famous climb up the highest mountain in the world, Mount Everest in the Himalayas. In 1953, Hillary and his Sherpa companion, Tenzing Norgay, were the first people ever to reach the summit of this towering mountain.

After conquering Everest, Hillary was knighted by Queen Elizabeth II. He then continued his explorations, including a 1958 expedition to Antarctica and the South Pole.

Since the 1950s, Hillary has lectured widely and written several books about his experiences. He helped establish assistance projects for the people of Nepal, the country where Mount Everest is located. Numerous schools, hospitals, medical clinics, and bridges have been built in Nepal with his generous support. Through his example, Sir Edmund Hillary hopes to encourage the spirit of adventure and peace in many young people of the world.

Feature Films and Art Exhibits

In recent years, New Zealand has made serious efforts to introduce the work of its artists to a wider audience. Some of the country's major films and art exhibitions have been shown throughout the world. Many have won high praise and awards.

The first New Zealand feature film to be shown in the United States was Roger Donaldson's 1977 movie, *Sleeping Dogs.* Donaldson used grant money from the Queen Elizabeth II Arts Council to produce his movie about a country fighting to free itself from a brutal police force. In 1981, he followed this successful film with another, *Smash Palace*, which tells the story of a family struggling through a divorce. Although set in New Zealand, the story told in the movie could take place anywhere.

New Zealander Geoff Murphy directed a movie about a subject unique to his homeland. Murphy's 1984

film, *Utu*—a Maori word for "revenge" or "payment"—
is set in the time of the Land Wars. When it was shown
at the Cannes Film Festival in France, *Utu* received
high praise. Some of New Zealand's best movies are
now shown on U.S. television and are also available on
videocassettes.

In the mid-1980s, American museum-goers were
given the chance to learn more about New Zealand. Between 1984 and 1986, an exhibition of classical Maori
art toured the United States. The exhibition, titled *Te
Maori*, opened at the Metropolitan Museum of Art in
New York City. It included 175 valuable, sacred pieces
such as wood carvings and weapons, dating from A.D.
1000 to 1880. Because the pieces held deep spiritual
meaning for the Maori people, forty-six Maori elders
accompanied the exhibition to perform special protec-
tive rituals to guard the mana of each item.

A Wealth of Vacation Fun

While *Te Maori* provided many Americans with
their first close look at New Zealand and the Maori
culture, other Americans know the country from first-
hand experience. New Zealand's stunning scenery and
beautiful cities make it a popular American choice for
foreign travel. Tourism is now a large part of New Zealand's economy. In 1987, more than 760,000 overseas

A scene from the 1984 New Zealand feature film, Utu.

Two young tourists enjoy a cruise on New Zealand's Milford Sound fiord.

visitors vacationed in the country, backpacking, boating, and skiing. Most of New Zealand's tourists come from Australia, the United States, and Japan, and many say they never want to leave. Some visitors do decide to stay in the country and start a new life—Europeans and others often see life in New Zealand as a chance to breathe clean air and live in harmony with nature.

New Zealand is a small country, but its size has not prevented it from accomplishing a great deal. Its people successfully run a government, protect the environment, contribute to the arts, sports, and industry, and preserve a unique cultural heritage and language. These achievements attract and inspire many people from all parts of the world.

Appendix

New Zealand's Embassies and Consulates in the United States and Canada

New Zealand's embassies and consulates offer assistance and resource information to Americans and Canadians who wish to learn more about this island nation.

U.S. Embassy and Consulates

Los Angeles, California
New Zealand Consulate General
10960 Wilshire Boulevard,
  Suite 1530
Tishman Building
Los Angeles, California 90024
Phone (213) 477-8241

New York, New York
New Zealand Consulate General
630 Fifth Avenue, Suite 530
Rockefeller Center
New York, New York 10111
Phone (212) 698-4680

San Francisco, California
Trade Commission and Tourist/
  Publicity Office
Citicorp Center
1 Sansome Street, Suite 810
San Francisco, California 94104
Phone (415) 788–7444

Washington, D.C.
Embassy of New Zealand
37 Observatory Circle, N.W.
Washington, D.C. 20008
Phone (202) 328-4800

Canadian Embassy and Consulate

Ottawa, Ontario
Embassy of New Zealand
Suite 801, Metropolitan House
99 Bank
Ottawa, Ontario K1P 6G3
Phone (613) 238-5991

Vancouver, British Columbia
New Zealand Consulate General
701 West Georgia Street, Suite 1260
IBM Tower
Vancouver, British Columbia
  V7Y 1B6
Phone (604) 684-2117

Glossary

Aotearoa (A·oh·TEE·ah·ROH·ah)—Maori name for the country also known as New Zealand

hangi (HAHN·gee)—a pit dug in the earth and used as an oven

huia (HOO·yeh)—a black bird, extinct since 1907; its white-tipped tail feathers were prized by Maori leaders

kumara (KOO·mah·rah)—a sweet potato

mana (MAH·nah)—influence, prestige, authority, or psychic force

maori (MAH·oh·ree)—normal or usual

Maori (MAH·oh·ree)—the name now used by the original people of New Zealand

Maoritanga (MAH·oh·ree·TAHN·gah)—the Maori culture or identity

marae (mah·RYE)—the space in front of a meeting-house

moa (MOH·ah)—a large flightless bird, now extinct

moko (MOH·koh)—the pattern of a tattoo

Pakeha (PAH·kee·hah)—a foreigner or white person

patu (PAH·too)—a short club used as a weapon

paua (POW·wah)—a shellfish with a colored shell, similar to an abalone

pipi (PIH·pee)—a small shellfish, like a clam

pohutakawa (POH·hoo·tah·kah·wah)—a tree native to New Zealand; it blooms with bright red flowers at Christmastime

poi (POY)—a ball covered in flax with a cord attached; it is swung and twirled by dancing girls or women

taniwha (TAN·ee·wah)—a type of water monster in Maori legends

tapu (TAH·poo)—sacred or restricted

toheroa (TOH·eh·roh·ah)—a type of clam usually made into a dark-green soup

utu (OO·too)—payment or revenge

Selected Bibliography

Ball, John. *We Live in New Zealand.* New York: The Bookwright Press, 1984.

Chavasse, P. G. R. and J. H. Johns. *New Zealand Forest Parks.* Wellington, New Zealand: P. D. Hasselberg, 1983.

Fingleton, David. *Kiri: A Biography of Kiri Te Kanawa.* London: Collins, 1982.

Graham, J. C., ed. *Maori Paintings by Gottfried Lindauer.* Auckland, New Zealand: East West Center Press, 1965.

Hillary, Sir Edmund. *Nothing Venture, Nothing Win.* New York: Coward, McCann & Geoghegan, 1975.

Jacobs, Warren, and John Wilson. *The Birth of New Zealand: A Nation's Heritage.* Auckland, New Zealand: Kowhai Publishing, 1985.

King, Michael and Martin Barriball. *New Zealand in Colour.* Wellington, New Zealand: A. W. & A. H. Reed, 1982.

King, Michael. *Maori: A Photographic and Social History.* Auckland, New Zealand: Heinemann Publishers, 1983.

McGuire, Edna. *The Maoris of New Zealand.* New York: The Macmillan Company, 1968.

Turnbull, Michael. *The Changing Land: A Short History of New Zealand.* Auckland, New Zealand: Longman Paul, 1975.

Williams, Herbert W. *A Dictionary of the Maori Language.* Wellington, New Zealand: A. R. Shearer, 1975.

Index

About the Author

Free-lance writer Valerie Keyworth immigrated to New Zealand with her family when she
was seventeen years old. She
lived there for eight years, receiv-
ing her bachelor's degree from
the University of Auckland. Today, she frequently returns to
New Zealand for extended vis-
its. Ms. Keyworth is a member
of the Society of Children's
Book Writers and volunteers her time for the California Liter-
acy Campaign. *New Zealand: Land of the Long White Cloud* is
her first book for children.

Ms. Keyworth currently lives in California with her hus-
band. She is working on a young adult novel to be set in New
Zealand.